The Magnificent Seven were like a family.

These girl gymnasts knew each other's strengths and weaknesses. They learned how to trust each other, push each other, and cheer each other on. Most of all, they learned how to be a team.

When the 1996 Olympic Games started, they were ready.

This was their chance to make history. No American women's gymnastics team had ever placed first in this competition.

The Magnificent Seven had one mission: win Olympic gold.

The most exciting, most inspiring, most unbelievable stories . . . are the ones that really happened!

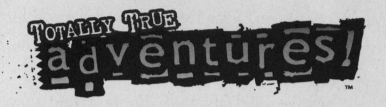

The $25,000 Flight
Apollo 13
Babe Ruth and the Baseball Curse
Balto and the Great Race
Climbing Everest
The Curse of King Tut's Mummy
Finding the First T. Rex
Kerri Strug and the Magnificent Seven
The Race Around the World
The Search for El Dorado
The Titanic Sinks!

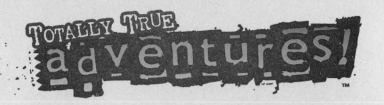

KERRI STRUG
AND THE MAGNIFICENT SEVEN

How USA's gymnastics team
won Olympic gold . . .

by Kaitlin Moore
illustrated by Michele Amatrula

A STEPPING STONE BOOK™

Random House 🏠 New York

Photograph credits: Cover photographs: Kerri Strug © Mike Powell/Getty Images Sport/Getty Images; Team USA, 1996 Summer Olympics © Peter Read Miller/Sports Illustrated/Getty Images; Bela Karolyi © IOPP/AFP/Getty Images; Dominique Dawes © Ales Fevzer/CORBIS. Interior photographs: pp. 88, 91, 100: © PCN photography/Alamy; p. 98 © AP Photo/Susan Walsh.

All rights reserved. Published in the United States by Random House Children's Books, a division of Penguin Random House LLC, New York.

Random House and the colophon are registered trademarks and A Stepping Stone Book and the colophon are trademarks of Penguin Random House LLC.

Visit us on the Web!
SteppingStonesBooks.com
randomhousekids.com

Educators and librarians, for a variety of teaching tools, visit us at RHTeachersLibrarians.com

Library of Congress Cataloging-in-Publication Data is available upon request.
ISBN 978-0-553-52174-0 (trade) — ISBN 978-0-553-52175-7 (lib. bdg.) —
ISBN 978-0-553-52176-4 (ebook)

Printed in the United States of America
10 9 8 7 6 5 4 3 2 1

This book has been officially leveled by using the F&P Text Level Gradient™ Leveling System.

CONTENTS

Guide to Gymnastics Events   vi

July 23, 1996   1

1. Growing Up Nadia   5
2. Whatever It Takes   13
3. The Champion Maker   19
4. Bela's Girls   24
5. The Road to the Olympics   30
6. Team USA   36
7. Setbacks and Comebacks   43
8. Back Together Again   52
9. The Magnificent Seven   61
10. Going for the Gold   66
11. Vaulting to Victory   74
12. Heroes Come Home   81

The Story Behind the Story   92

Glossary   96

Guide to Gymnastics Events

At every competition, women gymnasts compete on four events. In 1996, each gymnast could get a score from 1.0 to 10.0 for her routine. Now scores are based on a new system and are usually between 14.0 and 17.0.

Balance Beam

The gymnast moves up and down the beam while doing leaps, flips, and other moves. She must not lose her balance.

Floor

The gymnast does tumbles, jumps, and other moves on a large padded mat.

Uneven Bars

The gymnast swings and flips between the low bar and the high bar.

Vault

The gymnast must run, jump, and vault off a springboard. She must land on both feet on the other side.

Kerri Strug stood at the end of the runway. She was waiting for the green light. In gymnastics, green means go. As soon as it flashed, she would start running toward the vault, eighty-two feet away. Kerri had done this vault a hundred times. But this time was different.

This time her vault would make history.

Kerri was only eighteen years old, but she had a big job. She was representing the United States at the Olympic Games. She and her teammates were called the Magnificent Seven. That's because they were the strongest American women's gymnastics team in history. No American gymnastics team had ever won Olympic gold. None had even come close.

Until now.

The Americans were only one vault away from a gold medal.

It was Kerri's vault. It was her big chance to win victory for her team and her country. She had to do the vault perfectly. And she had to do it in front of the whole world. Thirty-two thousand people were watching her from the stands. Millions more were watching from home.

Each gymnast got two tries on the vault. Kerri had already used up her first try. She'd fallen hard and twisted her ankle. Pain went through her leg. She could barely feel her foot.

"Shake it out!" her coach told her. "Give me one last vault."

He knew the American team had no other choice. Kerri knew it, too. If she couldn't vault, it was all over. Everything was up to her.

For fourteen years, Kerri Strug had cared about almost nothing but gymnastics. She had worked hard. She had given up time with friends and family. She had battled through injuries and pain. Only one thing would make it all worth it: winning Olympic gold.

This was the moment she'd been waiting for her whole life. Did she have what it takes?

You can do this, she told herself. *You* must *do this.*

The green light flashed.

Kerri began to run.

1

GROWING UP NADIA

Kerri fell in love with gymnastics when she was four years old. That's when she started going to the gym with her big sister, Lisa. Lisa was twelve years old, and she loved showing off for little Kerri. She taught Kerri to do the tricks that the big girls did. At home, Lisa and Kerri did handstands and back handsprings across their backyard. Kerri couldn't wait until she was old enough to take lessons.

Lisa, Kerri, and their brother, Kevin, grew up in Arizona. Their house was filled with gymnastics. All three kids took lessons, but no one loved the sport as much as Kerri. She turned her whole world into a gym! Every curb was a balance beam. Every swing set was a bar to swing on. She even cartwheeled her way through cleaning her room.

When Kerri was seven, Lisa spent the summer in Texas. She trained with the most famous gymnastics coach in the world. His name was Bela Karolyi. Kerri and her parents went down to visit Lisa. They were amazed by what they saw. Lisa was working with the country's top gymnasts. That night Lisa taught Kerri some new moves. They used their hotel mattress as a gym mat.

The next morning, Kerri went back to the gym. It was full of girls training for gymnastic competitions. These girls spent almost every hour in the gym. Kerri wanted to be one of them. She knew this was where she belonged.

She wasn't the only one who noticed.

That day, an assistant coach asked Kerri's father if he would send her to Houston. The coach was sure Bela could make Kerri a star. Kerri had what it took to be the best.

"We'll take very good care of her and make her a champion," the coach promised.

Kerri's dad didn't stop to think about it. "Absolutely not," he said.

Kerri's parents were proud of her. But she was still very young. They didn't want her to move so far away. So Kerri and her parents went back home. But Kerri kept training. She couldn't get enough gymnastics.

A year before, Kerri had watched the 1984 Olympics over and over again. Women gymnasts compete on four events: bars, beam, floor, and vault. This is called the all-around, because they move from one event to another, "all around" the gym. Kerri watched them all. She memorized every gymnast's name and every routine.

She thought, *Someday that will be me.*

***

Gymnastics was a popular American sport in 1984. There were more than 150,000 kids training in gymnastics. Just like Kerri, many of them dreamed of competing at the Olympics someday. But until that year, no American woman had ever won a gold medal in gymnastics.

Then along came a young gymnast named Mary Lou Retton. She changed everything.

As a little kid, Mary Lou Retton was a ball of energy. Her mother used to call her the Great

Table Smasher and Lamp Toppler. All that energy was tough on the living room furniture, but it made her a great gymnast. She entered her first competition when she was eight years old.

Gymnastics scores go from 1.0 to 10.0. Ten is the highest score a gymnast can get. Little Mary Lou Retton's first score was 1.0.

She was proud and thrilled ... because she had read the scoreboard wrong. She thought she'd gotten got a ten!

After that day, she worked even harder. Her coach, Bela Karolyi, helped her. Mary Lou promised herself she would get better. *Much* better. And she did. She got *so* much better that she made the 1984 Olympic team.

The Olympics were in Los Angeles that year. The hometown crowd loved Mary Lou Retton. So did the judges. By the time she was through with bars and beam, she was almost tied for first place.

Then came the floor exercise. The "floor" is

actually a forty-foot square mat. The gymnasts twirl and flip and tumble across the mat. Mary Lou Retton was very good at her floor routine. But to have a chance at the gold medal, she needed to perform the best routine of her life.

And she did. She scored a perfect 10.0!

The crowd went wild. Mary Lou knew it wasn't good enough. Not yet.

She had one event left. It was the vault. To win, she needed to score *another* 10.0. That seemed impossible.

Gymnastics is all about doing the impossible. And Mary Lou Retton was the best gymnast in the world. She did score another perfect ten and won the individual all-around gold medal. She became the best American gymnast in history. After that, every young gymnast in America wanted to be just like her.

* * *

Kerri watched Mary Lou Retton's gold medal routines so many times that she memorized all her scores. In fact, she memorized *every* American score. Mary Lou Retton was soon Kerri's second-favorite gymnast.

Who was her all-time favorite? A Romanian gymnast named Nadia Comaneci. Kerri wasn't the only one who loved her. Nadia was Mary Lou Retton's favorite, too!

Nadia was one of Coach Bela Karolyi's very first gymnasts. Before he came to America,

Bela lived in Romania. In 1976, he coached the Romanian Olympic gymnastics team, and Nadia was his star. She was only fourteen years old. But she tumbled and flipped and vaulted like nothing the world had ever seen. After her uneven bars routine, the judges posted her score. It broke the scoreboard.

Nadia had won the first perfect ten in gymnastics history. Then she did it again, on the uneven bars. And *again* on the floor. She scored a total of *seven* perfect tens. She won the all-around gold medal. She became a superstar.

Kerri Strug knew all of that. She knew everything there was to know about Nadia. She even wore her hair in pigtails like Nadia did. Kerri wanted to be just like Nadia. She wanted to make Olympic history, too. And she promised herself that someday she would.

No matter what.

2
WHATEVER IT TAKES

A great gymnast needs a great coach. Kerri started serious training at the Tucson Gymnastics Center. Her coaches were Ellen Hinkle and Don Gutzler. Ellen and Don took her to her first big competition at Arizona State University. Kerri won first place in the ages nine to eleven group—even though she was only eight years old!

Kerri kept getting better, and a coach named Jim Gault started to notice. He coached college students at the University of Arizona. But he couldn't stop thinking about Kerri Strug. The nine-year-old tumbled like a champion. He knew he could help her get to the top. So he volunteered to start coaching her. It was exactly what Kerri needed.

Gymnasts compete in levels. The top level is called Elite. That's where Kerri wanted to be. Jim Gault was the man to take her there.

She worked hard to get ready for her first major meet. It was the Junior B American Classic. Nine-year-old Kerri would compete against girls who were twelve and thirteen. That didn't scare her. She was ready.

Then everything changed. One day in practice, Kerri fell on the vault.

Gymnasts fall all the time. But this time was different. It hurt to breathe. Her parents rushed her to the doctor. He had bad news for them. Kerri had fractured a bone in her rib cage called the sternum. It would take six weeks to heal.

That meant six weeks out of the gym and six weeks away from her training. Even worse, it meant no American Classic.

Kerri was angry with herself for getting hurt. Instead of winning her first big meet, she had to watch it on TV.

Kerri pushed herself hard to get back in shape. Soon she was ready to compete again. She was ready to win. She entered meet after meet. Gymnasts can compete in individual or team competitions. Kerri loved both. She collected high scores and sped through the ranks. Kerri traveled all over the country and met other girls like herself, who loved gymnastics more than anything. In 1990, she even traveled to the Netherlands. For the first time, she competed in the red, white, and blue of Team USA.

Kerri knew this was the beginning of her road to the 1992 Olympics. She had two years to get in the best shape of her life and prove herself to the world. It all started here.

There was just one problem. Kerri was a shy, quiet girl. Even though she had been to many competitions, no one knew who she was.

As she warmed up for the meet, a reporter came over to her. "Who are you?" he asked. "Why are you here?"

"I'm Kerri Strug," she said nervously. "I'm here to compete."

She thought that was a good answer. But the reporter just had more questions.

"Why isn't Kim Zmeskal here?" he asked.

Kerri knew who Kim Zmeskal was. In 1990, *everyone* knew who Kim Zmeskal was. Like Kerri, she was a great gymnast. Unlike Kerri, she was confident and outgoing. She was already famous. She trained with Bela Karolyi. He wanted to send Kim to the Olympics. He thought she could be the next Mary Lou Retton. The world expected Kim to be a champion. Compared to her, Kerri felt like a nobody.

Sometimes people treated her like one.

"Why did America send *you*?" the reporter asked.

"I don't know," Kerri said in a small voice.

It didn't feel like the answer of a champion.

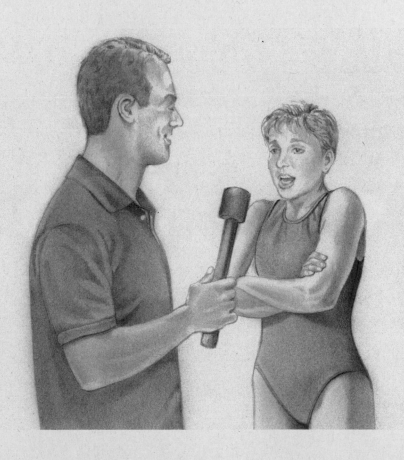

Kerri couldn't answer the reporter in words. Instead, she answered him in gymnastics. Why did America send her? Because she was strong and skilled and worked hard. Because she could *win.*

By the end of the meet, Kerri had scored third place in the all-around competition. She also got third place on floor and second place on bars and beam. She even beat the Romanian gymnasts. They were famous for being the world's best. After that, she wasn't a nobody anymore. Kids ran up to ask for her autograph. Kerri signed her name for them. It was her first taste of fame.

It tasted pretty good.

That was the turning point. When Kerri got home, she started looking for a new coach. She needed someone who could make her confident like Kim Zmeskal. She needed someone who could make her feel like a champion.

She needed Bela Karolyi.

3

THE CHAMPION MAKER

In 1990, Bela Karolyi was the most famous gymnastics coach in the world. He and Nadia Comaneci had been an amazing team in Romania. When she got famous, Bela got famous along with her. But life in Romania was hard. In 1981, Bela and his wife, Marta, moved to the United States. Marta was a gymnastics coach, too. They hoped to find new champions in their new country.

It wasn't easy. They had no gym and no gymnasts to coach. They had to start over again from scratch. But they loved gymnastics, and they loved training Olympic gymnasts. Soon Bela and Marta found a new superstar to train. Her name was Mary Lou Retton. After she won gold at the

1984 Olympics, many girls wanted to train with Bela. They all wanted him to make their dreams come true. Now Bela had plenty of students and a gym of his own in Houston. He even built a training ranch in the woods for his best gymnasts.

He called the ranch the American Dream.

* * *

Kerri Strug's dream was the 1992 Olympics. She knew Bela Karolyi was the one to make it happen. She just had to convince her parents that it was a good idea. It wouldn't be easy. Houston was a thousand miles away from home, and Kerri was only twelve. They hated the idea of sending her so far away.

But Kerri didn't give up. She wouldn't take no for an answer.

So she asked again. And again.

She begged them to understand. This was her best chance of making the Olympic team. Maybe it was her only chance.

Her parents didn't want to stand in her way. In December 1990, they agreed to let her follow her dreams.

Kerri and her mother were very close. Kerri told her everything, and her mother always knew how to make her feel better. In Houston, Kerri would be on her own. That year, Kerri asked for a journal for Christmas. She thought writing in the journal might feel like talking to her mother. And maybe she wouldn't feel so alone in Houston.

On Christmas, Kerri wrote in her brand-new journal: "Well, it's Christmas Day. I'm moving away for gymnastics.... I hope I'm doing the right thing."

By the next week, she was in Houston. Kerri was thirteen years old and four foot six inches tall. She had just made the most important decision of her life. She stood at the entrance of Bela and Marta's training gym. Had she made the right choice? She was about to become one of "Bela's girls." That's what the gymnastics world called them. The girls in this gym all wanted the same thing Kerri did. They wanted to make it to the Olympics. But not all of them would.

Bela's girls were the best of the best. Kerri watched them and worried. What if she didn't fit in? What if she couldn't stand being so far from her family? What if she just wasn't good enough?

She'd come this far. She couldn't turn back now.

Kerri stepped inside and into her new life.

4
BELA'S GIRLS

Lots of gymnasts trained at Bela's gym. Only the seven best got to train with Bela himself. One of them was Kerri Strug. She was the smallest and the least experienced. It was hard not to feel behind. But Kerri didn't let that stop her. She worked hard to catch up.

She worked harder than she ever had in her life.

Bela's girls got to the gym before sunrise. Their workouts were planned down to the minute. Even water and bathroom breaks were on Bela's schedule!

The morning session started with conditioning. *Conditioning* means exercises that get your

muscles in shape. Every day, the girls ran the length of the gym and sometimes they even ran backward. They did squat jumps and sit-ups. Sometimes they did three hundred of them at a time! Next, they did compulsories. *Compulsories* are a type of gymnastic routine in competitive meets. In a compulsory event, every gymnast performs exactly the same routine.

Ten-thirty was schooltime. Many gymnasts were homeschooled. Not Kerri Strug—her parents wanted her in class with other kids. They hoped that would remind Kerri there was life outside the gym. From 10:30 to 2:30, Kerri went to school. She took tests. She ate in the cafeteria. She gossiped in the halls. She did everything the other kids did. But after school, most other kids went off to play sports or watch TV. Kerri went back to the gym.

Afternoon training was for learning new tricks and working on optional routines. *Optionals* are the opposite of compulsories. Every gymnast makes up her own routine. Bela's girls trained until nine o'clock. Sometimes they stayed even later to work one-on-one with Bela or Marta.

Kerri went to the gym almost every day. She had no time for a normal teenage life. No time for parties or dances or pizza nights. Kerri didn't care about any of it. She was doing the best gymnastics of her life. Nothing else mattered.

Kerri wrote in her diary as much as she could. One day she wrote: "My back is sore, my stomach has a pulled muscle, my heel is bruised, and my legs are really sore. But I'm doing well, even though everything hurts."

She was always tired. She was always in pain. She got more homesick every day. She called her parents as much as she could, and her friends sent her care packages. But she missed seeing their faces. She felt very alone. Some nights she even thought about quitting.

But every morning, she went back to the gym. Then she remembered why she was there and why it was worth it. She would push herself just a little harder for just a little longer. The national championships were coming soon. Next would come the world championships ... then the Olympic trials. She was so close to her dream. She just had to hold on.

Bela Karolyi liked to make his gymnasts compete against one another. He set up pretend meets that worked just like real ones. Many times, Kerri won first place. She even beat Kim Zmeskal and Betty Okino. They were two of the country's most famous gymnasts. But could she do the same thing in a real competition, with real judges and a real audience?

Kerri was confident inside Bela's gym. But once she was out in the world, her nerves came roaring back. Bela called her his little bird because she was so shy. He called Kim Zmeskal his little lion. Kim was tough, and she didn't let any-one forget it.

The national championships were filled with reporters. They watched Kerri tie Kim Zmeskal for the best all-around optional score. Kerri also became the national champion on the vault. The reporters barely noticed. They only cared about Kim. She was the superstar. She was the Olympic favorite. Kerri was just the little bird.

She was getting tired of it.

5

THE ROAD TO THE OLYMPICS

Bela's girls had six weeks until the world championships. He took his four best gymnasts to train at his ranch. That way, they could spend all their time on gymnastics. They didn't do anything but train. They didn't talk to anyone but each other.

In August 1991, their hard work paid off. Bela's girls competed in the trials for the world championships. Only seven gymnasts could make it onto the US team—but all four of Bela's girls got a spot!

The 1991 world championships was the biggest, most important meet of Kerri's life so far. She'd trained hard. She was the best she had ever been. So was the rest of the team. Working together, they won the silver medal! The Soviet team won gold. This was no surprise. The Soviet gymnasts were the best in the world. No one could beat them, and it seemed like no one ever would.

Kerri was the youngest gymnast at worlds, but Kim Zmeskal was still the one in the spotlight, especially after Kim won the individual all-around competition. It was the first time an American scored at the top.

Bela reminded Kerri that winning wasn't just about talent. It was also about attitude. He told a reporter, "Right now, Kerri is saying, 'Yes, world, look at Kim. Don't look at me.'"

There were six months until the Olympic trials. That was where the country's best gymnasts would compete for a spot on the Olympic team. Only seven gymnasts would get chosen. Kerri was determined to be one of them.

Bela Karolyi was pretty determined, too.

In December, he decided that his girls should train through the holidays. That meant staying in Houston for Christmas. It was Kerri's first Christmas without her family.

She hoped it was worth it.

The girls worked harder than ever. Finally, the big day arrived. May 14, 1992, the US national championships. This was the first step toward getting picked for the Olympic trials. Only the top fourteen gymnasts would be allowed to compete in the trials. This was no problem for Kerri Strug. She came in second place!

Kim Zmeskal came in first.

Kerri tried not to compare herself to Kim. She tried not to think about anything but making the Olympic team. The trials were in Baltimore. Her whole family came to watch her compete. Even her older sister, Lisa, came. Lisa skipped her college graduation so she could cheer on Kerri.

"I have dreamed of this day since I was eight years old," Kerri wrote in her diary. "I've moved away from home, haven't had much of a social life, and have sacrificed so much. All to come down to this one meet. Crazy, huh?"

Kerri came in third place—she made the team! Or so she thought.

That year, many of the country's top gymnasts were too injured to compete in the official trials. So the United States of America Gymnastics organization (USAG) decided to have a *second* Olympic trials.

The top gymnasts went to Florida. They performed their routines for the USAG officials. There were no scores. No way of telling whether you were winning or losing. All you could do was hope that the USAG thought you were Olympic material.

Kerri hoped. Kerri prayed. She thought about her ten years of hard work. She thought about everything she had given up. If they called her name, she would get to join Team USA. She would have her chance at Olympic gold.

If not, her Olympic dream would be dead.

Finally, it was time. The USAG announced the

Team USA lineup for the 1992 Olympic Games.

Shannon Miller. Kim Zmeskal. Dominique Dawes. Michelle Campi. Wendy Bruce. Betty Okino.

And Kerri Strug.

The 1992 Olympics took place in Barcelona, Spain. Every Olympics begins with an Opening Ceremony. The host country puts on an amazing show that includes its history and culture. Hundreds of people work to entertain the crowd and honor the athletes. Each country's team marches into the ceremony wearing their national colors. They hear the cheers of hundreds of thousands of people. For many athletes, this is the first time the truth finally sinks in.

I am at the Olympics. I made it.

Kerri Strug and the rest of the Team USA gymnasts watched the ceremony on TV. The gymnastics team competition would start early the next morning. Bela Karolyi was the team's head coach. He thought they needed their rest more than they needed the spotlight.

The next morning, Kerri and the others reported to the gym. They nervously waited for their turn on the mat. First up were Team Compulsories. Then came Team Optionals. Those scores would decide which team won the gold. They would also decide which gymnasts got to compete for individual medals.

Kerri planned to make the cut. She had competed with her team in so many world competitions. But she had never made it into the individual all-around. This time she had to. Most gymnasts retire after going to one Olympics. This could be her only chance.

The world's eyes were on Team USA. Most especially, they were on Kim Zmeskal. Everyone expected her to bring home the gold. She leaped onto the balance beam for her first routine. She

moved gracefully through her familiar twists and turns, and then...

The impossible happened.

Kim Zmeskal, superstar gymnast...fell off the beam.

The crowd couldn't believe it. Neither could Kim. The fall didn't just drop her score, it shook her confidence. Only the top three gymnasts from each country would get to enter the individual all-

around. Her chances had just gotten much worse.

Kerri's chances, on the other hand, had just gotten much better. She tried not to think about it like that. All that mattered now was the team competition. To win that, they all had to be strong.

Sometimes one gymnast's mistake can rattle a whole team. Team USA wouldn't let that happen. They'd worked too hard. So they shook off Kim's fall. They showed the world what they could do.

What could they do? They performed so many nearly perfect routines that they ended the day in second place. They were just behind the Soviets and ahead of the Romanians!

Day two was Optionals, when the gymnasts got to perform the routines they made up themselves. When the day started, Kerri was in thirteenth place. She knew she had to be one of the top three US gymnasts. That meant hitting every routine and sticking every landing. She told herself: "You can, and you will."

And she did.

The world was watching. This was the most important competition of her life. But Kerri didn't flinch. She hit every routine. She stuck every landing. But she still didn't make it into the individual all-arounds! She missed out by 0.014 of a point.

She lost to Kim Zmeskal.

In the final scoring, Team USA came in third place. That meant Team USA got to stand on the podium. Everyone on the team got a bronze medal. It should have been the happiest night of Kerri's life. Instead, she cried herself to sleep. The individual competition would start the next day, but Kerri's Olympics were over. In her diary, she wrote, "I got an Olympic medal and I'm miserable. This is the most upset and disappointed I've ever been."

Kim Zmeskal didn't win the all-around. She didn't even get an individual medal. Instead, Ukrainian gymnast Tatiana Gutsu won the all-around gold. Shannon Miller took silver. Shannon won many more individual events and came home with five medals total. She was the hero of the Games. Kerri was overlooked once again.

Then she got even more bad news: Bela Karolyi was retiring! He and Marta left Spain as soon as the medals were handed out. Kerri didn't even get to say goodbye.

He was the best coach she'd ever had. She didn't know how she could replace him. Or if she wanted to. The Olympics were her dream, and now they were over. Kerri had accomplished her life goal. But she was only fourteen years old.

What was she supposed to do next?

7

SETBACKS AND COMEBACKS

After the Olympics, Kerri traveled across Europe with her family. It was the first real vacation she'd taken in years. She thought hard about what she wanted to do with her life. Fourteen years old seemed so young to retire. But it wasn't just that. She couldn't imagine giving up gymnastics. She loved it too much to stop. And she still dreamed of winning an *individual* Olympic medal.

Which meant she needed to find a new coach.

That was harder than it sounded. Kerri visited gyms all over the country. She was looking for one that felt like home. She ended up at Brown's Gym near Orlando, Florida. This was the gym where the Olympic trials had been held. It felt lucky. At least, it did at first.

Kerri never felt at home there. Soon she decided it was time to move on. She tried Steve Nunno's gym in Oklahoma City. Steve was Shannon Miller's coach. Bela Karolyi and Kim Zmeskal had both retired. That made Steve and Shannon the new superstar duo.

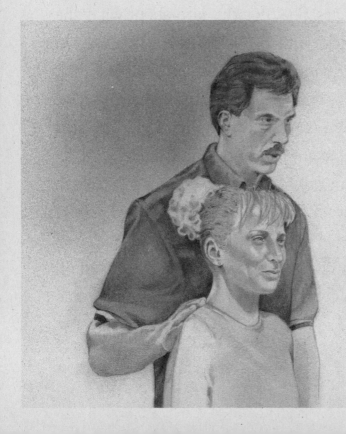

Shannon and Kerri pushed each other to be better. And Steve Nunno pushed them both hard. He wanted to prove he was just as good a coach as Bela. Maybe even better.

In 1993, Kerri made it to the world championships again. *International Gymnast Magazine* later said, "Anyone familiar with the sport knows Strug was the top tumbler there."

But somehow even her best wasn't good enough to qualify for the individual all-arounds. She lost out to a young gymnast named Dominique Dawes by only 0.1 of a point. Kerri was furious. She couldn't believe this had happened *again.*

By 1994, Kerri was sad and frustrated. No matter how hard she worked, it wasn't enough. She was pushing herself harder than ever. It was doing more harm than good. One day she pulled a stomach muscle. That was her body's way of telling her to slow down. Kerri didn't listen. She trained through the pain until the muscle couldn't take it anymore. It tore in the middle of a competition. The pain was so bad that Kerri lost focus. When she leapt off the beam, she landed on her face.

It was the lowest moment of her gymnastics career. Something had to change.

Kerri packed her suitcase and left Oklahoma behind. She went home to her family. It took six months for her stomach muscle to heal. While she waited, Kerri tried to forget about gymnastics. She tried to live a normal teenage life.

She thought it would be impossible. But it was amazing.

Kerri discovered that there was a whole world outside gymnastics. She saw old friends and had fun with her family. She ate pizza and went to the movies.

She was finally happy again. Slowly, she was getting herself back into shape. She started off just doing simple tricks like cartwheels and handstands. At first, that was all her body could handle.

Kerri worked with a coach named Artur Akopyan. He helped her return to gymnastics in a healthy way. Unfortunately, he lived in California, and Kerri didn't want to leave home again. What could they do?

Her parents and Artur Akopyan came up with a plan. He would stay in California, and Kerri would stay in Arizona. The coach would fly to Arizona and train Kerri whenever he could. It wasn't easy, but they made it work.

Training with Artur was different from training with Bela or Steve. There was no Kim Zmeskal, no Shannon Miller. This time Kerri was the only world champion in the gym. She had no one to compete with. No one but herself.

She liked it that way. It helped her remember what she loved about gymnastics. It didn't have to be about winning. It could be about doing your best. Making your body do the impossible.

Kerri took her time. She wanted to do things right. But finally, she felt ready to enter a major competition. She picked the US Classic for her big comeback. She would be competing against some of the new generation of gymnasts: Amy Chow, Jaycie Phelps, and Amanda Borden. Dominique Dawes, from 1992's Team USA, would be there too. These were the girls Kerri would be competing against for a spot on the 1996 Olympic Team. If she made it that far.

First, she had to prove herself at the US Classic. She was confident. She was ready. And she started off strong. Her floor routine was graceful. Her vault was powerful.

Then came the uneven bars. From the start she could feel something was off. Her rhythm felt wrong. The swings and flips didn't flow right. She wasn't swinging high enough or

powerfully enough. There wasn't anything she could do except try to make it through without disaster.

Then, as she was swinging into a handstand, her hands slipped.

She smacked her face into the low bar and fell to the ground.

She fell hard.

Pain shot up her back. This hurt like she had never hurt before. Something was very, very wrong.

"Help me," she whispered. "Somebody help me."

The crowd fell silent. A trainer warned her not to move. But Kerri couldn't move. She was in too much pain.

She was too afraid.

Her parents rushed to join her. An ambulance rushed her to a hospital. There, doctors X-rayed her back. Kerri knew back injuries can be very serious.

She didn't know if she would ever do gymnastics again.

She didn't know if she would ever *walk* again.

She tried to be brave for her mom and dad.

They tried to be brave for her. Finally, the doctor came into the room. He was holding an X-ray of Kerri's back. Kerri's parents asked him how bad it was. Kerri could hear the fear in their voices.

They all knew his answer could change everything.

8
BACK TOGETHER AGAIN

Kerri had a stress fracture in her back. She would heal completely. Kerri's parents breathed a huge sigh of relief. But not Kerri. She knew this meant more recovery time. And that meant more time out of the gym. She'd worked so hard to get back into shape. Now she had to start over again from the beginning?

The stress fracture needed six to eight weeks to heal. And it hurt a *lot*. Kerri wore a back brace to keep her spine steady. Some days it felt like she would never get better. But time passed, and slowly but surely she got better. She healed quickly enough to compete in the 1994 world championship trials, and she made Team USA!

The championships were in November. Kerri was strong ... but she was also nervous. She couldn't stop thinking about what had happened at her last competition.

Slipping.

Falling.

Landing hard. The explosion of pain.

For the first time in her life, she was afraid of gymnastics.

When it was her turn, Kerri stared up at the uneven bars. She told herself she could do it. She'd done it so many times before. She was good enough. She was strong enough. She just had to be brave enough.

She took a deep breath and leapt for the bars. Her hands tightened around the bar. Her body swung into motion. As it did, her fear flew away. Her body knew what to do. She swung and flipped and turned through a smooth, powerful routine. At the end, she landed surely on her feet.

It was the beginning of an amazing competition. Kerri and her teammate Dominique Dawes led the American team to a team silver medal.

Kerri Strug was back.

In June 1995, Kerri graduated from high school. Now she had the time she needed to train for the Olympic trials. She had the strength. She just didn't have the coach.

Then Kerri heard an amazing rumor.

Bela Karolyi was returning to coaching.

Kim Zmeskal was coming out of retirement. She wanted to make another Olympic team. A very young, very talented gymnast named Dominique Moceanu had the same hope.

Bela agreed to coach them both. Kerri thought: *Why not me, too?*

Soon she was back in Houston, back in Bela's gym.

She knew right away: *This is where I belong.*

Bela was the same as she remembered.

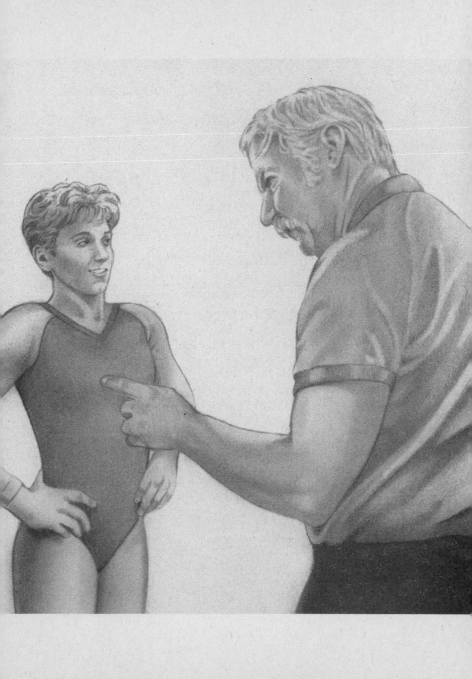

Kerri was very different. She was older now. More important, she was *confident*. She wasn't Bela's little bird anymore. She was a lion now. She was ready to roar.

No coach ever pushed her like Bela did. He taught her some amazing new tricks. The hardest one was a vault called the Yurchenko one-and-a-half twist. This vault started with a run down the runway at full speed. Then came a round-off onto the springboard. From there, a gymnast flipped onto the horse, pushed off her hands, and did a one-and-a-half twist in the air before landing.

If Kerri could pull off the vault in competition, she would be unstoppable.

It was March 1996. Olympic trials were coming up fast. Kim Zmeskal realized she wouldn't be strong enough in time. She went home. Now it was just Kerri and Dominique.

The national championships were in June.

Only the top fourteen gymnasts would get to compete at the Olympic trials.

Dominique Moceanu was only fourteen years old. She'd been the youngest national champion in history. She would be the youngest member of the Olympic team ... if she made it. But Dominique had a stress fracture in her leg. Kerri had some pain in her shins. Would they let a little pain stand in their way? Not a chance. They both qualified for the Olympic trials.

Usually gymnasts compete for one of seven spots at the trials. This year Shannon Miller and Dominique Moceanu were injured. They couldn't compete. The USAG let them use their scores from nationals to qualify for the Olympics. That left only five spots on Team USA.

Kerri wasn't worried. Not this time. She'd finally found her confidence—and it showed. Her shins were still hurting, but she pushed

Kerri
Strug

Shannon
Miller

Jaycie
Phelps

Amy
Chow

through it. She came in first place in the all-around optionals!

For the second time in her life, Kerri heard her name announced at the Olympic trials. She was going to the 1996 Olympics. So were Amanda Borden, Amy Chow, Dominique Dawes, Shannon Miller, Dominique Moceanu, and Jaycie Phelps.

Dominique
Moceanu

Dominique
Dawes

Amanda
Borden

Bela told *Sports Illustrated* that this was the strongest team the United States had ever sent to the Olympics. Shannon Miller's coach, Steve Nunno, agreed. "We finally have a team that has the opportunity to win the gold medal," he said. "If we hit all our routines . . . there's nobody that can beat us."

9
THE MAGNIFICENT SEVEN

It *was* the strongest American women's gymnastics team in history. Sports reporters called them the Magnificent Seven. Everyone believed they had what it took. They would go to the Olympics and bring home the gold.

After their months of training, Kerri and Dominique Moceanu knew each other inside and out. But who were the other five girls? What kind of teammates would they be?

Amanda Borden grew up and trained in Cincinnati with her coach Mary Lee Tracy. She came very close to making the 1992 Olympic team, but she got cut at the last minute. "I can't really explain what making the team means to me after just missing in 1992," Amanda told a reporter. Then she changed her mind. She *could* explain: "Dreams come true. That's what it means." Amanda was the team captain.

Amy Chow was from California. She had competed in her first international competition only two years before. At her first world championships, she helped her team to a silver medal. No Asian American woman had ever won an Olympic medal in gymnastics. Amy wanted to be the first.

Dominique Dawes was nineteen years old, the oldest on the team. She had fifteen national titles and had competed in three world championships. She was also Kerri's teammate on the 1992 Olympics team. When Dominique was very young, she took a crayon and wrote the word *determination* on her mirror. She wasn't just determined, she was talented. As she grew up, she earned the nickname Awesome Dawesome.

Shannon Miller was the only American in history to win a gold medal at worlds twice in a row. When the 1992 Olympic Games began, she was in Kim Zmeskal's shadow. By the end of the competition, she was a superstar. She brought home four individual medals. Four years later, she hoped to prove she was still on top.

Dominique Moceanu was born in Romania. She reminded many people of Nadia Comaneci. Like Nadia, she was very young, very small, and very talented. But she still had a stress fracture in her leg. She would be strong enough to compete. But would she be strong enough to win?

Jaycie Phelps almost quit gymnastics when she was twelve years old. That year she placed twenty-fourth in the national championships. Instead of quitting, she switched to a new gym. The next year, she came in *sixth* place at

Nationals. Then she helped Team USA win a silver at the 1994 worlds. These Olympic Games were her chance to prove she belonged with the best of the best.

The Magnificent Seven spent a week training together in Greensboro, North Carolina. That year, there were two Olympic team coaches: Mary Lee Tracy and Marta Karolyi. By the time the week was over, the girls were like a family. They learned each other's strengths and weaknesses. They learned how to trust each other, push each other, and cheer each other on. Most of all, they learned how to be a team.

When the Games started, they were ready.

The 1996 Olympics were held in Atlanta. From day one, the American women gymnasts were the superstars of the Games. Reporters wanted to interview them. Photographers shoved cameras in their faces. Fans begged for autographs. But the coaches didn't want anything to distract the team. So instead of staying in the Olympic Village with the other athletes, Team USA stayed in a secret hideout. They had a cook, a security team, and a private bus to take them to the gym. And they had a mission: win Olympic gold.

10

GOING FOR THE GOLD

The Olympic team competition stretched over two days. Day one: compulsories. Day two: optionals. The scores at the end of these two days would decide which team took home a medal. It would also decide which gymnasts got to compete for individual medals. Again and again, Kerri Strug had missed the cutoff for the individual all-around. This time she wasn't going to let that happen.

Every gymnast at the Games wanted to earn the chance to win an individual medal. But for those first two days, they had to focus on being part of a team.

Only six countries had teams strong enough

to seriously compete for gold: the US, Russia, Romania, Ukraine, Belarus, and China.

Until the 1992 Olympics, Russia, Ukraine, and Belarus were all part of one country called the Soviet Union. For forty years, the Soviet women's gymnastics team won gold at every Olympics except the 1984 Games. (That year, the Soviet Union didn't enter.)

In 1991, the Soviet Union broke apart into separate countries. Now Russia, Ukraine, and

Belarus were competing *against* each other. Together, they might have been unstoppable. But for the first time in forty years, the US, China, and Romania had a real chance at gold.

The Romanians were used to coming in second place to the Soviets. They were tired of it. Many gymnastics experts thought this was their year. But right before the Games started, two members of their team were injured and couldn't compete. Another gymnast was still recovering from surgery. And the team leader had a sprained ankle! It wasn't the best way to start the competition.

China had put together their strongest team ever. All but one of the Chinese gymnasts was a member of the 1995 world championships team, which took home a silver medal. They were led by a superstar named Mo Huilan, who was nicknamed China's Little Angel. The Chinese team came to Atlanta hoping to make history.

One day of compulsories. Four events. Every

routine mattered. Every gymnast knew: *This is it. The moment I've worked toward my entire life. The moment that counts.*

Team USA marched into the stadium and the crowd rose to its feet. The applause was like thunder. Thirty-two thousand people can make a lot of noise.

Coaches Marta Karolyi and Mary Lee Tracy huddled with their team. They were full of last-minute advice. The gymnasts' personal coaches had plenty to say, too, but they weren't allowed on the main floor. They had to stay up in their seats. That didn't stop them. Bela Karolyi and Steve Nunno leaned over the railing as far as they could and shouted advice.

All the training paid off. The Magnificent Seven performed one amazing routine after another. The only event that gave them any trouble was the balance beam. They were a little nervous. And on the beam, nervousness works against you. Jaycie Phelps, who started out a little shaky, even fell off midroutine.

Fortunately for the Magnificent Seven, all the other teams had just as much trouble. Compulsories can be very hard for gymnasts, and beam compulsories can be the hardest of all. (Kim Zmeskal had fallen off the beam in her 1992

Olympic compulsory routine. She never got her confidence back.) This may be why international competitions have since gotten rid of them. The 1996 Games were the last Olympics with compulsory routines.

After the beam, the Americans came back strong. They performed beautiful floor exercises. Dominique Moceanu was still battling a stress fracture in her shin, but she earned a 9.750. It was the highest score of the day so far. Shannon Miller was up next. She had tendonitis in her left wrist, but she tumbled like she could feel no pain. She earned a 9.787.

Olympic judges often give lower scores to the gymnasts who perform first. This is why coaches save the strongest competitors for the end. On floor, Kerri Strug tumbled last and earned a 9.825. That was a high enough score to put the Americans in the lead.

Their final event was the vault, and Team

USA did even better on that. Once again, Kerri Strug went last. She earned an amazing 9.812!

The Americans beat the Ukrainians, Belarusians, and Romanians. China went next, but they couldn't catch up with Team USA.

No American team had ever finished the compulsories in first place. The Magnificent Seven watched the Russians compete. They held their breath. Would the Russians take the lead?

At practice, the Russians had looked weak. The gymnasts made one mistake after another. Every routine was off, and every landing was wobbly. But in competition? They were almost perfect.

One Russian gymnast after another pulled in huge scores. Even the beam gave them no trouble. They flew to the top of the scoreboard. With their very last vault, they pulled ahead of Team USA.

The day ended with the Americans in second

place. They were ahead of the Romanian team, but 0.127 behind the Russians. They had one day of competition left. They still had a chance to beat the Russians. But they would have to do the best gymnastics of their lives.

11

VAULTING TO VICTORY

The Olympic team gymnastics finals were held on July 23, 1996. This was the Magnificent Seven's chance to make history. That morning, Kerri wrote herself a message in her journal: "Kerri, you can and you will have an outstanding performance. Show the world how hard you've worked."

On the ride to the gym, no one spoke. They were too nervous. Once they got there, Dominique Moceanu grinned at her teammates. There was a fierce look in her eyes. "Let's hit everything," she told them.

They did.

It was the kind of day gymnasts dream of.

Every routine was smooth. Every landing was solid. Every score was high. Slowly but surely, the Americans took the lead. The Ukrainians and Belarusians fell far behind. China slipped down to fourth place. The Romanians clawed their way to third. By the last event, even the Russians had fallen behind.

Team USA couldn't believe it. With only one event left, they were in first place! They were so far ahead that only disaster could knock them out. The Russians went into their final event certain they had lost. Their star gymnast burst into tears before her floor routine. That's how sure she was that the Americans would win.

All Team USA had to do was get through their last event, the vault. It should have been easy. The vault was one of their best events. They felt very confident. Then Dominique Moceanu raced down the runway, flipped over the vault . . . and fell.

The crowd gasped. Dominique was supposed

to be the star of the Games. How could she fall?

Each gymnast got two chances to try her vault. The lower score wouldn't count. So Dominique shook herself off. She took a deep breath and raced down the runway again. She leapt onto the vault, flipped and tumbled through the air . . . and fell *again*.

The crowd was shocked. So were the Magnificent Seven. The Russians were thrilled. Did this mean they actually had a chance to win?

The Russians and the Americans were competing at the same time. Russia was on floor while Team USA was on vault. Each gymnast tried to focus on her own routine. But it was hard to ignore the scores from the other side of the gym.

Especially when Kerri Strug stepped to the edge of the runway. This would be the final vault of the day. Kerri was doing the Yurchenko one-and-a-half twist. It was the most complicated, highest-scoring vault she had ever done in competition. If she could pull it off, Team USA would win gold.

She *knew* she could pull it off.

"Hit this," she told herself. "Hit this vault."

She ran down the runway. She hit her round-off hard, bounced off the springboard, and somersaulted onto the horse. And then... disaster. Her rhythm was a split second off. When you're moving that fast, a split second is everything. Kerri pulled her arms in too soon. She hit the floor before she was ready and slammed into the ground.

She felt something snap.

It was her ankle, and it was throbbing with pain.

Kerri massaged her foot. She tried to force the pain away. She still had to do her second vault. And this one had to be perfect.

"You can do it!" Bela cried from the stands.

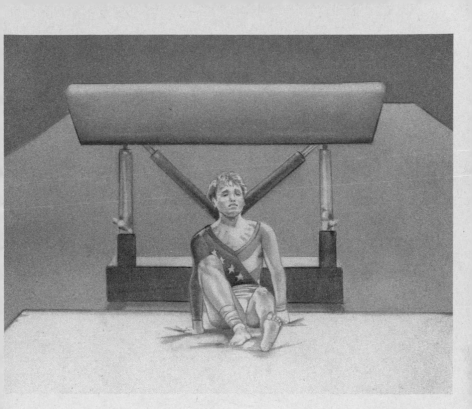

"You can do it!" Marta could see Kerri's foot was hurting and urged her to shake it out.

Kerri's foot had gone numb. Something was very wrong. But she *had* to make it through this vault. She couldn't let her team down.

She couldn't let her country down.

She stood at the end of the runway. *You can do this, Kerri. You must do this.*

The green light flashed, the light that meant: *Go.*

Kerri ran at the vault. Her feet pounded against the runway. She refused to think about her ankle. She refused to feel the pain.

She kept her eyes on the vault. She kept her mind on her goal.

She ran.

As hard as she could. As fast as she could. She hit the round-off at exactly the right moment. She slammed her hands against the vault, then pushed herself into the air. She flipped upside down, completing the one-and-a-half twist. Then her feet rocketed into the floor. Pain exploded up her ankle and through her body. Kerri ignored it.

She stuck the landing.

For one brief second, she stood straight and proud, with both feet on the ground. Then she lifted her injured foot. She hopped on the good one and saluted the judges. The vault was officially over. The pain came flooding back.

Kerri collapsed.

She couldn't move. She couldn't do anything but cry with pain. But she was still thinking about the vault. *Did I do it?* she wondered. *Was it good enough?*

The crowd started to clap and stomp their feet. The noise was louder than thunder. It was the sound of 32,000 people cheering with excitement. Kerri's score had come in: 9.712.

It was enough. It was *more* than enough. For the first time in history, the United States women's gymnastics team won Olympic gold.

Kerri had made history.

Team USA had proven they were the best gymnasts in the world. It was time to step onto the podium to collect their medals. But Kerri was in too much pain to get up. How was she supposed to walk up the stairs of the podium? How could she stand there while the national anthem played and the judges placed a gold medal around her neck?

But how could she miss the moment she'd been waiting for her entire life?

"Even if I have to carry you, you're going out there," Bela promised her. And that's exactly what he did.

Bela scooped Kerri into his arms. He carried her to the platform. She stood proudly beside her teammates, balancing on one leg. The crowd cheered, "USA! USA! USA!" They were so proud of their hometown girls. Then the arena fell silent. "The Star Spangled Banner" boomed over the speakers. As the music played, Kerri stopped thinking about the pain. For a few minutes, she was too happy to think about anything but that

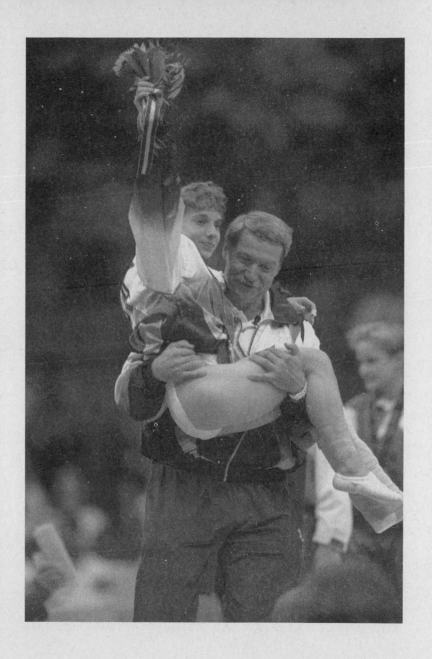

gold medal around her neck. Everything else fell away.

When the ceremony ended, Dominique Moceanu and Shannon Miller helped Kerri hop off the podium. They were still teammates. They would always help each other.

Kerri was so happy for her teammates. But there was a big question on her mind. Would her ankle heal in time for the next day's individual events? Her team scores where high enough to qualify for the all-around. *Finally.* What if she was too injured to compete?

Kerri took an ambulance to the hospital. The doctors checked her out. Then they gave her some bad news. Her ankle was seriously injured. She definitely couldn't compete in the all-around. Kerri's Olympics were over.

The doctors bandaged her up and sent her back to her team. That's when she found out she was famous. People all over the world had watched her vault on TV. They thought she was a hero. Even the president called her on the phone to thank her!

But that night, Kerri cried herself to sleep. She would never win an individual medal at the Olympics. That day, she'd made one dream come true. But because of it, her other dream was lost.

For the next few days, Kerri watched her team from the sidelines. It was triumph after triumph for the Magnificent Seven. Shannon Miller won the gold medal for her beam routine. Amy Chow took the silver on the uneven bars. She was already the first Asian American woman to win an Olympic gymnastics medal. Now she had two. Then Dominique Dawes made history again to become the first African American to win an individual gymnastics medal when she got the bronze for floor. Kerri cheered them on.

She didn't blame her teammates for what happened. She didn't blame anyone. But she

couldn't stop wondering, *what if?* What if she had gotten to compete? Would she have beat out Romanian gold-medal winner Simona Amanar on vault? Was she a match for Ukraine's Lilia Podkopayeva, who won the all-around gold? She would never know.

And maybe that was okay.

Kerri gave everything she had to her team. She helped them make history. She was coming home with an Olympic gold medal. She was a national hero.

After the Olympics, the Magnificent Seven were famous. They went to the White House and met the president. Their picture was on a Wheaties box! They were stars, and Kerri was the brightest star of all. She had spent her whole gymnastics career in someone else's shadow. Not anymore. Now *Kerri* was in the spotlight. *Sports Illustrated* called her vault "the most memorable athletic moment" of the Olympics.

Bela told the magazine, "She is just a little girl who was never the roughest girl … always a little shy, always standing behind someone else. But sometimes this is the person with the biggest grrrrr."

Bela's little bird was now a lion, and the whole world knew it. Kerri was always quick to remind reporters that she was part of a team. She knew every girl on the team would have done exactly the same thing as she did. Amy, Shannon, Jaycie, Amanda, and both Dominiques had all worked just as hard as Kerri. They all loved gymnastics just as much. They were all willing to do anything to become Olympic champions. All seven girls had spent years proving that to their coaches, their parents, the judges, and themselves. On July 23, 1996, they proved it to the world. Millions of people watched Team USA battle their way to victory and learned the truth. These seven girls truly were magnificent.

THE STORY BEHIND THE STORY

KERRI STRUG
AND THE MAGNIFICENT SEVEN

Where Are They Now?

AMANDA BORDEN owns a gym of her own, where she's training a new generation of champions.

AMY CHOW made it to the 2000 Games in Sydney. She's now a pediatrician who helps injured young athletes get back on their feet.

DOMINIQUE DAWES went to the 2000 Olympic Games, too. In 2010, President Obama appointed her as co-chair of the President's Council on Fitness, Sports, and Nutrition.

SHANNON MILLER battled cancer in 2011. Now healthy again, she works to give women the information they need to lead healthy lives.

DOMINIQUE MOCEANU retired from gymnastics in 2006. She is the author of four children's books about gymnastics, the Go-for-Gold Gymnasts series. She also wrote a book about finding her long-lost sister—who is a gymnast too!

JAYCIE PHELPS started her own gym. It specializes in cheerleading, baseball, softball, soccer, and, of course, gymnastics.

KERRI STRUG graduated from Stanford University, then moved to Washington, D.C., where she spent a few years in public service. She is a spokesperson for several charities, including the March of Dimes. She has no regrets about her Olympic vault. "When you sacrifice so much and you finally do well," she says, "it feels really good."

The Next Generation

It took sixteen years for the United States to win another women's gymnastics team gold medal. In 2012, Gabby Douglas, McKayla Maroney, Aly Raisman, Kyla Ross, and Jordyn Wieber competed for Team USA at the London Olympics. They nicknamed themselves the Fab Five.

"We are definitely the fiercest team out there," McKayla Maroney said. She was right. The team beat Russia for the gold and took home four more medals for individual events. Gabby Douglas became the first African American woman to win a gold medal in the individual all-around. Once again, Team USA made history. It surely won't be the last time.

GLOSSARY

balance beam—one of four events in women's gymnastics. Gymnasts dance and tumble across a long, narrow beam. The beam is 16 feet long, 3.9 inches wide, and 4.07 feet high.

compulsories—the part of a competition where gymnasts are assigned a routine. Every gymnast performs the same one.

conditioning—exercises that get your muscles in shape

floor—one of four events in women's gymnastics. Gymnasts tumble and flip across a 40-foot square mat.

individual all-around—the part of a competition where gymnasts compete for themselves instead of the team. They move "all around" the gym and compete on four events: bars, beam, floor, and vault.

Olympic Games—an international sports competition that takes place every four years, in summer and winter. Gymnasts compete at the summer games.

Olympic trials—where American gymnasts compete for a spot on the Olympic team

optionals—the part of a competition where gymnasts perform routines they made up themselves. Every gymnast does something different.

runway—the long, narrow carpet a gymnast runs down on her way to the vault. It is always 82 feet long.

Soviet Union (USSR)—a country that no longer exists. Russia, Belarus, and Ukraine all used to be part of it.

Sports Illustrated—a popular American magazine about sports

stress fracture—tiny breaks in a bone that happen over a long period of time. This often happens to athletes who are pushing too hard.

uneven bars—one of four events in women's gymnastics. Gymnasts swing and fly between two bars. One is high (8 feet off the ground). One is low (5.5 feet off the ground).

United States of America Gymnastics (USAG)—the organization that makes the rules for US gymnastics and picks the Olympic team

vault—one of four events in women's gymnastics. Gymnasts vault over a padded leather platform 4.5 feet off the ground. It is sometimes called a horse. Gymnasts run down a runway, hit a springboard, then spring onto and over the horse.

Get ready for more

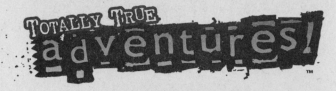

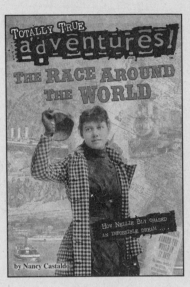

Nellie Bly had an amazing idea. What if she tried to go around the world in less than eighty days? In 1889, people said it could not be done—especially by a woman. But soon the whole world was rooting for her! Could she make it back home in time?

Available now!

Crack! An edge of ice split off and dropped into the deep dark hole. Hillary fell. He tried to slow himself by jamming his boots into the icy wall.

"Tenzing!" he shouted. "Tenzing!"

In a flash, Tenzing plunged his ice ax into the snow. He wrapped his rope around the ax to hold it steady. Then he threw himself on the ground, to anchor the rope even more.

The rope tightened. Hillary jerked to a stop. He was fifteen feet down, far into the crack of ice. Bit by bit, he pulled himself up. His gloves were torn, and his body was bruised. But he was alive.

New friends. New adventures.
Find a new series . . . just for you!

BALLPARK *Mysteries*
FOR THE SPORTS FAN

THE DINO FILES
FOR THE ADVENTURER

Louise Trapeze
FOR THE SUPERSTAR

PIPER GREEN
FOR THE DREAMER

PUPPY PIRATES
FOR THE ANIMAL LOVER

Totally True Adventures!
FOR THE EXPLORER

RandomHouseKids.com